MY CLASS
AT
DIWALI

MY CLASS
AT
DIWALI

Ruth Thomson
meets
Samantha Zeglicki

Photography: Chris Fairclough

Franklin Watts
London/New York/Toronto/Sydney

We are trying on our costumes.
Tomorrow, our class is doing a play
to celebrate Diwali.
Diwali is the Hindu festival of lights.

We have done all sorts of work
about light and shadow.
We measured our shadows at different times.
We cut out shadow pictures.

We talked about things which give light.
We made pictures of bonfire night.

On the night of Diwali,
some people light candles in their houses.
I am decorating a candle
with shiny stars and sequins.

Other people light diwas,
which are clay lamps,
with cotton wool wicks dipped in oil.
My friends are making potato prints of diwas.

Diwali marks the end of the Hindu year.
People send cards to wish their friends
a happy Diwali.
We make some cards of our own.

People also decorate the entrances
to their houses with Rangoli patterns.
Mrs Thakrar helps Michael and Kamaran
to chalk a pattern outside our classroom.

We make our own Rangoli patterns
on squared card.
We glue coloured rice, lentils and sand
on the squares.

People offer sweets
to friends and relatives at Diwali.
Mrs Thakrar shows us
how to make some.

We decorate the sweets with nuts.

All our work is put up in the hall
to decorate it for our Diwali assembly.

DIWALI
FESTIVAL OF LIGHTS

It's time to get ready for the play.
Mrs Murray pins my sari in place.

Neil makes
fierce noises
behind his demon
king mask.

Michael helps Chris
with his crown.

The whole school comes to watch.
Our mums and dads have come as well.

First we sing a Diwali song.
The band plays tambourines and jingles.

Now it's the play.
Tom tells the story of Ram and Sita.

"There was once a king who had three wives.
The wives all had sons.
One of the sons was called Ram.

"A few miles away, lived a princess called Sita. She had an enormous bow. She would only marry the prince who could string her bow.

"Many princes came to try their luck,
but none of them could even lift the bow.
Ram came and lifted the bow easily.
He managed to string it.

"So Ram and Sita were married.
They went home to see the king.
The king said, 'I am getting old now.
Ram can be king in my place.'

"Ram's step-mother was jealous.
She said to the king, 'You owe me two wishes.
I want my own son, Bharat, to become king.
I want Ram to go away for fourteen years.'
The king had to agree.

"Ram and Sita went to live in the forest.
Sometimes Ram went hunting.
He left Sita in a magic circle to protect her.
Ravan, the wicked demon king, came.
He tricked Sita into stepping out
of the circle.

"Ravan took Sita to Lanka, his kingdom.
Ram searched everywhere for her.
On the way, he met Hanuman, the monkey god.
The monkeys helped Ram to fight Ravan
and rescue Sita.

"Ram took Sita home.
Everyone lit lamps and decorated their houses
to welcome them back.
This is why candles are lit at Diwali.
Ram and Sita became king and queen."

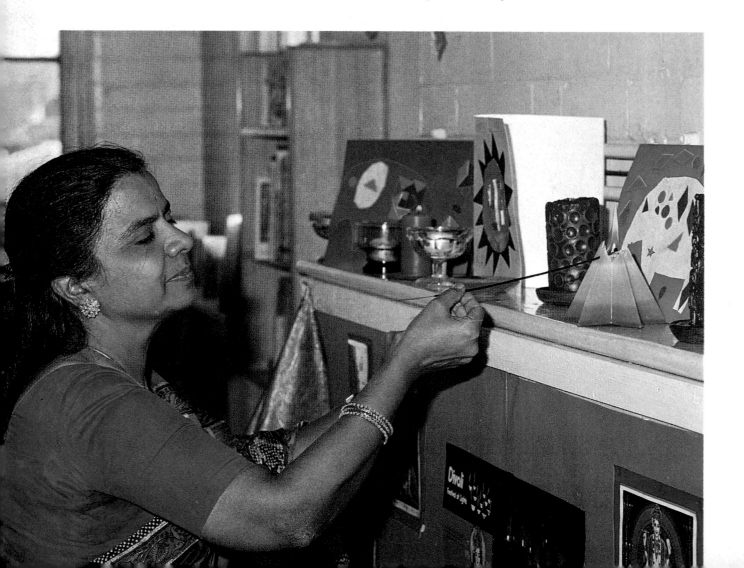

After the play, we give our mums and dads
some Diwali food.
We wish everyone happy Diwali.

૨૦૪૧
2041

આસો વદ   November

30   12

મંગળવાર   Tuesday

દિવાળી
Diwali
1985

૨૦૪૨
2042

કારતક
સુદ   November

૧   13

બુધવાર   Wednesday

નૂતન વર્ષાભિનંદન
Happy New Year
1985

© 1986 Franklin Watts Limited
12A Golden Square
London W1R 4BA

ISBN   0 86313 425 4

Printed in Italy

The Publishers, author and photographer
would like to thank the staff and pupils of
Musters Road County Infants' School, West
Bridgford, Nottingham. Special thanks are
due to Phyl Cooper, the Head teacher, Jenny
Murray and Pushpa Thakrar.

Ruth Thomson is a freelance editor and
writer of childrens' books.